MEMOR
BRIS'

Part of the
MEMORIES *series*

Contents

First published in Great Britain by True North Books Limited. England HX3 6SN. 01422 244555.
www.truenorthbooks.com. Copyright © True North Books Limited, 2012

ISBN 978 - 1906649807. Text, design and origination by True North Books
Part of the 'Memories' compact series and based on the original Memories of Bristol publication.

Memories are made of this

Memories. We all have them; some good, some bad, but our memories of the city we grew up in are usually tucked away in a very special place in our minds. The best are usually connected with our childhood and youth, when we longed to be grown up and paid no attention to adults who told us to enjoy being young, as these were the best years of our lives. We look back now and realise that they were right. So many memories - perhaps of the war and rationing, perhaps of parades, celebrations and Royal visits. And so many changes; one-way traffic systems and pedestrianisation. New trends in shopping led that to the very first self serve stores being opened.

Through the bad times and the good, however, Bristol not only survived but prospered. Fine old buildings continue to dominate the city centre, and besides the many monuments and sites of historical interest which have been preserved and restored. None of the city's experiences have gone to waste; instead they have combined to make Bristol such an interesting place, full of character. We have only to look at the city as it is today, with its finest buildings now cleaned and restored to their full glory, and the traditional tourist attractions now complemented by up-to-the-minute facilities, to see what progress has been realised and what achievements have been made. So sit back and enjoy the ride, as we take you on a pictorial meander through the streets of our great city.

Events and occasions

The poor of Bristol - many of them unemployed - had much to thank the Prince of Wales for back in the early 1930s, when people were still suffering from years of national depression and long-lasting unemployment that had marked the previous decade. A national Unemployment Fund had been created in 1928 - the 'dole' of a pitiful sum that was barely enough to keep alive on, yet infuriating to the well-to-do who saw it as encouraging laziness. The Prince of Wales took a personal interest in the plight of the men who were out of work and their families who never had enough to eat.

Prince Edward visited Bristol on 6th November 1934, and this photograph captures some of the exuberance of the welcome he was given by Bristol families, many of whom would have benefited from his help. He succeeded to the throne on the death of his father George V in January 1936, and renounced the throne on 10th December the same year for the American divorcee Wallis Simpson, 'the woman I love'.

Can I have a ride, Dad?' A seat on the elephant's swaying howdah, far above the ground, was one of the excitements to be looked forward to on a visit to Bristol Zoo. This photograph dates from 1936, and the name of this patient elephant is not known. Rosie, however, joined the zoo two years later, and thrilled every child who rode around the zoo on her back until she died in 1961.

When Clifton Zoo was opened in 1835, its founders had serious study and scientific research on their minds rather than amusement. They soon found themselves in financial difficulties, however, and they realised that the zoo's survival depended on finding commercial attractions that would entice the public to spend money there. In 1859 a balloon ascent would have set you back a shilling, with a concert thrown in for good measure. In more recent years the BBC's Natural History Unit used Clifton Zoo in its films, featuring the popular presenter Johnny Morris, who died in 1999.

MEMORIES OF BRISTOL

Bristol, never slow to recognise the opportunity to party, had pulled out all the stops to celebrate the coronation of King George VI, our present Queen's father, on 12th May 1936. Beneath the streamers, garlands and bunting that waved gaily in the breeze, the Official Souvenir Programme went on sale around the city for the grand sum of twopence - affordable even by the poorest families. How many of these programmes survive? The photograph, taken in Corn Street near the nails, shows some of the decorations that were hung everywhere in the city in celebration.

King Edward abdicated when British protocol insisted that he could not marry Wallis Simpson, who was divorced, and his younger brother the Duke of York was obliged to step into his shoes.

The new King George VI, a shy family man, had never expected to take the throne, but he dutifully took up the reins of kingship, encouraged by his beautiful queen, today our much-loved Queen Mother, and went on to shepherd his country through the second world war and to become one of the most popular sovereigns in history.

Long live King George: Wine Street, along with the rest of Bristol streets, took on a carnival air in 1937 to mark the coronation of King George VI. Floodlighting was used for the first time, much to the amazement of Bristolians, and bunting, flags and garlands welcome the new monarch to the throne. A mere three years on Wine Street was in ruins and little was left of the buildings pictured. The King visited Bristol in 1940 to see the war damage for himself.

MEMORIES OF BRISTOL

Back in 1934 every child in Bristol knew that if you wanted to see the real Father Christmas, Brights store in Queen's Road was where you should go. A huge crowd, mostly composed of children, turned out on the 24th November to give the old guy a noisy and enthusiastic welcome to Bristol. Christmas started later in those days of widespread poverty and unemployment; how many of these children woke up on Christmas morning to find little or nothing in the stocking they had hopefully left out the night before? We would not wish for a return to the poverty of the 1930s - but oh, for those simple, non-materialistic Christmases!

With Santa in his open-top motor car were Robinson Crusoe and Man Friday, suitably dressed for the British winter in warm skins and fur caps. Too much realism, it was felt, might be rather chilly. Defoe's character Robinson Crusoe was based on the real-life sailor Alexander Selkirk, who was marooned for five years on the uninhabited Más a Tierra Island. Rescued by Bristol seaman Woodes Rogers, Selkirk arrived back in England in October 1711.

MEMORIES OF BRISTOL

It was an exciting day for everyone when cowboy superstar and stunt rider Tom Mix appeared in a variety show at the Hippodrome, and on 5th March 1939 crowds lined the streets of Bristol to catch a glimpse of the Hollywood hero, jostling for the best views. Many fans stood at upper windows to get a grandstand view, while children were the lucky ones, grabbing a seat on Dad's shoulders.

Mix's film career had started with the early silent films and had continued with the advent of the 'talkies' - a feat which was unusual in itself, as many of the stars of the day did not survive the transition. The Western gained popularity in the earliest days of the cinema, offering many imaginative story-lines to the film-maker.

The coronation gave everyone a chance to declare their loyalty to the Queen - and it was party time in Bristol. Garlands and banners were hung in windows, lines of bunting stretched across every street, and though the weather on the big day was inclined to be cool and rather damp, it didn't stop the children from enjoying their street parties. Judging by the piano and the stage that had been erected, a party was clearly planned for the residents of Dean Crescent in Bedminster. Their imaginative decoration of the street had been awarded second prize in the competition for the best-decorated street that was run by the Western Daily Press.

The pageantry of the coronation is well-remembered by those who were lucky enough to see the event on television; people who had no set of their own crowded into the parlours of their more fortunate neighbours. The sight of the new queen being anointed with oil and having the crown placed upon her head is one which few can forget.

Union Jacks flutter from every child's hand as well as from the upper windows of the George and Dragon. And what was all the excitement about? Princess Elizabeth was coming to town! Great crowds lined the roadside to cheer the beautiful 24-year-old as the royal car was driven through Bristol. Rooftops, were fair game if a way could be found to get up there, and the roofs of the brewery in Old Market Street, the Victoria Rooms and the Drill Hall were filled with people who were determined to get a bird's eye view of the procession. What a reception Bristol gave her! The entire route was alive with flowers and flags; girl guides, school children, senior citizens, telegraph boys and Red Maids waved their hats, Union Jacks, handkerchiefs, streamers, rattles, and anything else they could get hold of, and enthusiastic students dressed in Elizabethan costume formed a tableau beneath the word 'Gloriana'.

MEMORIES OF BRISTOL

It was 1951; the Festival of Britain was in full swing, and Bristol as usual was not going to be left out when it came to a celebration.

The Festival of Britain was staged to celebrate the original Festival of 1851. It was the brain-child of Prince Albert, Queen Victoria's consort, and the extravaganza, which promoted British achievements, was staged in the purpose-built Crystal Palace.

One hundred years on, several buildings were constructed to mark the Festival's centenary, including the prestigious Royal Festival Hall and an exciting structure called the Skylon, which rose 300 feet above the exhibition grounds; illuminated at night, the Skylon was visible for miles around. Britain had indeed achieved much - but as every Bristolian knew, there was some way to go before post-war prosperity was theirs, indeed some goods were to remain on ration for a further three years. The 3rd July 1954 was the day the nation had been waiting for; crowds of people who were sick and tired of coupons gathered in Trafalgar Square and joyfully tore up their much-hated ration books!

A fascinating photograph that raises more questions than it answers. A smartly dressed salesman has collared part of a bombed-out building in Fairfax Street to make himself a bob or two, though frustratingly we can't quite make out exactly what he was selling! Interestingly, men both old and young are in the majority in this group, though a few ladies can be seen on the outskirts of the action. Slick-talking salesmen have always been around to charm the pennies and shillings from people's pockets, and whatever was on offer, a few fivers (or perhaps tenners?) appear to be in the process of being handed over by punters eager to part with their cash.

This photograph was taken in 1955, and the cars in the background reflect the year. Mature readers will remember the old Ford Popular - and those vacuum wipers that gave up the ghost when you speeded up and flogged away like mad when you took your foot off! This site is today occupied by the Galleries Shopping Centre.

This massive crown was erected in the Centre Gardens to celebrate the Queen's coronation on 2nd June 1953. The elaborate decoration was a thing of beauty with its red 'velvet' and jewels, all set on a base of royal blue. But it was after nightfall that the crown came to brilliant life, when hundreds of coloured lights sparkled like gemstones in the darkness. The crown was later shipped off to Canada, and we are not aware of its eventual fate.

Unlike her father King George VI, Princess Elizabeth had begun her training for the throne early, when Edward VIII's abdication in 1936 made her the heir presumptive to the throne. She was only 14 years old when she broadcast messages of encouragement to the children of war-torn Britain, and as the war progressed she gradually took on more and more public duties.

MEMORIES OF BRISTOL

'Pick a Pye for Christmas' was the commercial message of these Father Christmases who paraded outside an electrical store in The Horsefair in December 1960. The goods these Santas had on offer were transistor radios - the latest thing in gifts in the 1960s. The popularity of these novel miniature radios quickly becoming all the rage, and no self-respecting teenager would be seen without his or her faithful 'tranny'! Pocket-sized transistor radios had been developed by the Japanese company Sony as early as 1952, though it took a few more years before they became available in Britain at a price that most people could afford.

The Horsefair and Broadmead were central to the enormous changes that had been made in Bristol after the second world war. Many old buildings that survived the bombing raids fell victim to the redevelopment and road building schemes of the 1950s.

Down by the riverside

The phasing out of Bristol's trams began in 1938, and removal of the lines was causing havoc at regular intervals around the city. Some cities, of course, simply covered them over with tarmac, but not Bristol, where the scrap metal value of the lines was recognised and appreciated.

When work began early in 1939 on taking up the tram lines on Bath Bridge, workmen's lorries took station in the middle of the road and long queues of traffic formed in either direction, as can be seen from this photograph, taken on 3rd March. The cyclist on the left would today be likely to be wearing a helmet, an innovation undreamed of back in the 1930s.

As the volume of traffic increased year by year, Bath Bridge was found to be inadequate to meet the growing need for wide roads that kept the growing number of vehicles flowing smoothly around the city. The situation was vastly improved by the addition of a second bridge nearby.

MEMORIES OF BRISTOL

Why was it that ice cream always tasted better when we were young? This ice cream seller near the corner of St Augustine's Bridge was caught on camera in June 1935, and he has quite a queue of youngsters to deal with, all hungry for their special treat. Every child's eyes are on his hands as he places a wafer in his mould, adds a scoop of ice cream, spreads it out and places another wafer biscuit on top. Today, it seems that wherever we live we cannot escape the jangling music that can be heard several times a day as the ice cream seller tours our streets. Today's kids have a wider choice, however, than these children had, as these up-to-date vans will provide them with ice lollies and cold drinks as well as several different kinds of ice cream.

MEMORIES OF BRISTOL

By the 1930s traffic congestion in the city of Bristol was becoming a real headache. The problem was acknowledged, though the creation of wider roads meant the demolition of many older properties, and in 1936 work began on cutting new roads across the city. In a dramatic move that was to change the appearance of the city centre for ever, plans were drawn up to cover in a stretch of the River Frome that from the 13th century had been a lively quay reaching into the city as far as Colston Avenue.

MEMORIES OF BRISTOL

Work began in 1936, though for months little appeared to be happening. Ships still tied up at St Augustine's Bridge, though their days were numbered. HMS Fortune and HMS Firedrake *(left)* saw the end of the line, and this photograph taken on 3rd July 1937 captured an important part of Bristol's history. By this time the Dublin shed had been demolished and the site used temporarily as a car park (though how the front row of cars escaped a ducking defies imagination!). By the following year the scheme to culvert the river was well underway *(above)*. Site huts are dotted here and there, while huge cranes dwarf the workmen.

MEMORIES OF BRISTOL

Things ancient and modern - and Brunel's beautiful Clifton Suspension Bridge contrasts strongly with the civil engineering schemes of a much later generation. Opened in 1965, the roads and bridges of the Cumberland Basin complex speeded the flow of traffic between Bristol and Weston via what was, at 860 tons, the largest swing bridge in Britain. Looking towards the city, the hallowed grounds of Bristol City Football Club lie just off the photograph to the right, while on the horizon lies the rather select area of Clifton Downs. But for the last 150 years it has been Clifton Suspension Bridge - the jewel in Bristol's crown - that has made the city memorable in the minds of thousands of visitors to the city. Isambard Kingdom Brunel was incredibly only 24 years old when he entered his design for a new bridge to span the Avon Gorge - and won the contract. Sadly he was never to see his beautiful creation as although the foundation stone was laid in 1831 construction work on the bridge did not begin until after his death in 1859.

Wartime

'If the gas rattles sound, put your gas mask on at once, even in bed,' government leaflets instructed the people of Britain during the Second World War. Mustard gas attacks had been feared, and 38 million masks had been distributed as early as 1938. But by 1940 gas fears receded and few people bothered to carry them around any more. When war broke out every effort was made to accustom children to the frightening and claustrophobic gas masks that made parents and friends look like fearsome monsters. The little boy on the left looks quite relaxed and confident wearing his mask, though the boy on the right of the picture doesn't seem quite so sure. Children had regular half hour gas mask drills in local community halls.

In 1939 Britain's Prime Minister Neville Chamberlain had made his announcement to the waiting people of Britain that '...this country is at war with Germany.' This time planes had the ability to fly further and carry a heavier load, and air raids were fully expected. Air raid shelters were obviously going to be needed, and shelters were built on open places across the town.

By the time war was declared an army of volunteers of both sexes had already been recruited to form an Air Raid Protection service. It was their job to patrol specified areas, making sure that no chinks of light broke the blackout restrictions, checking the safety of local residents, being alert for gas attacks, air raids and unexploded bombs. Older Bristolians will remember how difficult it was to find certain items in the shops during the war; combs, soap, cosmetics, hairgrips, elastic, buttons, zips - all were virtually impossible to buy as factories that once produced these items had been turned over to war work. Stockings were in short supply, and resourceful women resorted to colouring their legs with gravy browning or with a mixture of sand and water. Beetroot juice was found to be a good substitute for lipstick.

Clothes rationing was introduced in 1941, and everyone had 66 coupons per year. Eleven coupons would buy a dress, and sixteen were needed for a coat. The number of coupons was later reduced to 40 per person. People were required to save material where they could - ladies' hemlines went up considerably, and skirts were not allowed to have lots of pleats. Some found clever ways around the regulations by using materials that were not rationed. Blackout material could be embroidered and made into blouses or skirts, and dyed sugar sacks were turned into curtains.

Above: A proud father poses for the camera with his latest arrival. The baby had not arrived from Mars, in fact the 'arrival' was not a baby at all, but an anti-gas attack suit which was compulsory for babies in the United Kingdom during the Second World War. An air pump at the side of the suit enabled anxious parents to replenish the supply of air to the precious package inside. The picture was taken in 1939. In the event there was never any gas attack on British soil during the course of the second world war.

Those who did not go into military service of one kind or another worked in factories, dug for victory, gave up their aluminium baths and saucepans, joined organisations and aided in any way they could. These boys were not going to be left out; they might be too young to fight but while there were sandbags to be filled they were going to do their bit to protect their school building.

Left: Rotted sandbags meant holes to push your fingers through and lots of nice trickly sand to play with and to scatter around the pavement - if you were five years old, that is! When war broke out in 1939 the filling of sandbags became a priority, and even older school children helped out in the work of filling the thousands of bags needed around the city. Sandbags were piled high around every important building and every ARP post in Bristol, protecting them from bomb blast.

Piled up outside doors and windows, sandbags provided excellent cover from bomb blast and prevented windows shattering, and the owners of shops, offices, pubs and on occasions even private houses - like the one seen in this photograph - also resorted to sandbagging their premises. Other people stuck tape in criss-cross patterns across their windows or covered them with net - anything to prevent injury from flying glass in an air raid. Splinter-proof lacquer painted on windows was another favourite way to protect one's property.

Right: It was 8th May 1945, and Winston Churchill and President Truman had proclaimed VE Day. Out came the flags and the bunting, and this entire community in St Michael's Hill went wild with joy when the news that everybody was waiting for was announced. A toddler gazes up in wonder at the hated Adolph Hitler, whose effigy has been suspended high above the street. In the Pacific the war continued for a further four months; the Japanese surrendered on September 13th. When Bristol had had time to draw breath, there was much to be done to restore the city that had suffered such extensive bomb damage. Strange as it may seem, rebuilding started with demolition, and whole areas of the city were swept away in the name of progress. Housing was desperately needed, and new estates built in the 1950s included 15-storey blocks of flats, where few people from the old communities felt at home.

Soon after the outbreak of war in 1939, people were preparing for the worst. Volunteers of both sexes were urgently needed to fulfil all kinds of duties; Air Raid Precaution wardens were appointed, and men who were outside the age for military service joined the Home Guard. The Women's Land Army, the evacuation service, the Women's Voluntary Service and the Auxiliary Fire Service all sought recruits. Watched by a group of children who, it is hoped, did not go home soaked to the skin, these auxiliary firemen are practising their new skills in Stapleton Quarry. Their expertise was to be desperately needed during the horrific scenes of devastation that reduced huge areas of our city to rubble.

The National Fire Service took on the control of all civic fire brigades during World War II, and women as well as men worked for the NFS. Many women certainly acted as fire watchers; on occasions incendiaries fell into unattended office blocks and factories and started fires, many of them burning unchecked in city centre properties. Firewatching eventually became a compulsory duty, and all men between 16 and 60 were called on to organise a fire-watching rota. Later on women between 20 and 45 joined them.

It was April 1940, and though at home little appeared to be happening and people were talking about the 'phoney war', in Scandinavia things were hotting up and the war was far from phoney. Russia was invading Finland and Germany was planning a full scale invasion of Norway and Denmark (which was geographically in their way). Hitler was more than slightly miffed when ten of his destroyers, a heavy cruiser and a couple of light cruisers were all sunk, and other vessels badly damaged, an event that made headline news.

This newspaper seller had no way of knowing that seven months on war would have become a grim reality for everyone in Bristol, and that his patch on the corner of High Street and Wine Street was destined to disappear in the onslaught of enemy bombs. The Dutch House, seen in the background of this nostalgic photograph, was bombed on 24th November. How many readers will remember the well known larger than life tin soldier that used to stand on the balcony? He was rescued from the ruins and given a place in the City Museum.

During World War II the public were bombarded with slogans that rained down on them as thickly as German bombs: 'Dig for victory!'; 'Britain can take it!'; 'Careless talk costs lives'; 'Make do and mend'. The posters that were designed to boost morale and keep people security conscious appeared on every available advertisement hoarding. Rumour could spread panic like wildfire and was seen as a real danger, so the Air Raid Prevention wardens based in Brunswick Square decided to run a poster campaign of their own.

An all too common sight during the second world war - homes reduced to a pile of rubble by bombs, and families made homeless. This row of four houses in St Agnes Avenue suffered extensive damage in the blitz that wiped out many of Bristol's buildings on Good Friday 1941. People rescued what few pitiful belongings they could, and descended where possible on their relatives. Relatives, too, might have found themselves homeless however, and many bombed out families in Bristol had to find a temporary home in tents.

Readers with a sharp eye might pick out the barrage balloon on the left, flying in nearby Victoria Park. As soon as an air raid siren sounded it was time to fly the barrage balloons that had been placed in the most important areas around the city. When flying high over the city (the maximum flying height of the balloons was 6,000 ft), this ingenious form of defence prevented enemy planes from diving low over the streets to make close-up attacks.

MEMORIES OF BRISTOL

Below: Everyone loves a parade, especially when it is headed up by a band playing a rousing march, and huge crowds lined the streets of Bristol to watch this American regiment march down Park Street. They were no doubt delighted with the style of the American marching band. US soldiers were a familiar sight in the city; Clifton College, for example, was vacated during the war and the whole school evacuated to Bude, and American troops occupied the buildings from 1942. We have no firm date for this photograph, but the event is likely to have celebrated the end of the war, either on VE Day or perhaps VJ day on 20th August 1945. Could it perhaps have been part of the huge Thanksgiving Parade that staged in Bristol to mark VJ day?

Evidence of the wartime bombing raids can still be seen here on both sides of the roads. Thankfully the University Tower, seen in the background, survived. Built by the Wills family of tobacco fame as a memorial to their father H O Wills, the tower has been a familiar landmark in the city since it was completed in 1925.

Right: The war was over, and huge crowds gathered outside the Council House along Corn Street to hear the Lord Mayor, Cllr W F Cottrell, officially declare that the war in Europe had ended.

He made the announcement from the historic coach which only rarely sees the light of day, being reserved for special occasions such as the accession of a monarch to the throne, a coronation - or the end of a war.

Making a living

Agrim expression is on the face of this news vendor in the High Street (left), whose paper carries the latest news of Hitler's doings in Europe. It was 6th April 1940, seven months after Britain had declared war against Germany. These news headlines remind us that in Europe things were very different. Norway and Denmark lay geographically in the way of Hitler's plans, and on 9th April Germany invaded both countries. Before long the war would become a grim reality for the people of Bristol. The Angel Fountain, set into the wall of St Nicholas' Church, was later removed to a place of safety. St Nicholas' itself was one of the many places of worship that fell victim to enemy bombs. During the war, every day brought important news. 'Holland and Belgium Invaded' the Bristol Evening Post placard shouted on 10th May 1940, and even the news vendors stationed by the Angel Fountain have their heads deep in the newspaper, obviously worried about the implications of this particular item of news. It was Holland and Belgium's turn to hit the headlines; claiming that he believed that the British and French were making preparations to attack Germany through the Netherlands, Belgium and Luxembourg, Hitler had marched in to occupy the Low Countries, even though they had repeatedly declared their decision to remain neutral. Hitler claimed that he had 'irrefutable evidence' of Allied invasion plans. With the occupation of Belgium the Maginot Line was circuited and the door into France was wide open. The 4th June saw British troops hastily evacuated from Dunkirk back to Britain; by the 25th, fighting in France had ended. The 10th May was a key date in the 1940 calendar, and other news in this same paper would report that Chamberlain had resigned and that Winston Churchill

Just swanning along: An adventurous swan found itself under arrest in April, 1939, when it left its watery home to wander the streets of Bristol. It took the long arm of the law to capture the fugitive on Bristol Bridge. The swan had earlier been pursued along Victoria Street and into Redcliffe Street, providing an amusing diversion for passers-by. The incident was captured only months before the outbreak of the Second World War, when most of the buildings pictured were destroyed in air raids.

Around the city

The red pen of the city planners took over where the wartime air raids left off, and Bristol lost many of its surviving fine buildings in what the novelist J B Priestley once labelled 'Council vandalism'. Readers will perhaps remember the chemists Strode Cosh & Penfold and James Phillips furnishers in this shot of Union Street, captured in the late 1940s. The stores on the left fell victim to the redevelopment of the area, and in time were replaced by the Tesco Metro store, while the right eventually saw the building of the Galleries Shopping Centre. Beyond the Nelson Street and Broad Mead crossing, Broadmead Baptist Church can be seen in the distance on the right towards Horse Fair. Few things were sacred - even churches - and Broadmead Chapel, too, was demolished in the late 1960s and replaced by shops.

By the autumn of 1940 Britain had been at war for a year. Along with most other everyday commodities, petrol was strictly rationed - though who would think it, judging by the stream of traffic in College Green on this sunny day? Bristol, with the rest of the country, was preparing for air raids. With the street lighting gone for the duration of the war and headlights of all vehicles shaded, driving in the blackout was tricky. Many drivers resorted to painting the wings, front and rear bumpers and running-boards of their cars white in an attempt to avoid accidents - though many accidents did still happen. Note the shop windows on the far left, which have been taped over to minimise the effects of flying glass during an air raid, and the pedestrians dutifully carrying their gas masks. The tops of buses, normally painted white, were blackened during the war as camouflage during air raids. But very soon after this photograph was captured, the air raids were to become a grim reality.

MEMORIES OF BRISTOL

These views of Colston Avenue as it was in September 1949 will stir many memories - and perhaps renew a few sighs as we remember the lovely old buildings which survived the war only to fall victim to modernisation. On the corner of Clare Street a row of sun blinds protects the goodies in the window of Thornton's Chocolate Kabin; the elegant Sun building with its ornate columns and dome was destined to become the site for a tall office block. Nearby, the Dunlop building, which still had its unusual tower at the time of the photograph, was in time to become the Watershed Arts complex. Across the Centre Gardens, the bus company's booking offices still wore their 'olde worlde' look at the time of the photograph; it has now lost its impressive Tudor effect, though the clock remains.

There is little traffic about in the Centre in this memorable view, and the cyclist calmly hogging the middle of the road in the days long before cycle helmets were required, would appear to be in little danger. He is approaching the notorious 'scissors crossing' caused by a merging of traffic. In 1957 this large traffic island was removed. Readers may well have checked their watches by the clock on the old CWS building, a landmark which was also doomed to be replaced by a modern block - albeit still with a clock. Adverts, too, belong to the city's history, and the massive Table Waters sign by 'you know who' was part of our scenery for years.

With the Labour Exchange in Nelson Street to the left, where over the years thousands of luckless souls waited in dreary queues, the view - which has changed drastically over the last 30 years - looks from Myers' multi-storey car park towards Rupert Street. The year was 1964; building sites have been cleared, and within a few years construction work would begin on the Police Headquarters and the Magistrates' Court. The old Bridewell police station can be seen in the right foreground - and spot the old police Road Traffic Department, almost dead centre. The 150ft Cabot Tower juts into the skyline on the far left of this shot. The tower was built to commemorate the historic voyage of John Cabot, who set sail with his son Sebastian in 1497 in the 'Matthew' in search of a western route to India, landing in Newfoundland.

MEMORIES OF BRISTOL

It's when we see such a vista, captured from the University Tower in 1957, that we realise just how much the city has lost. Fry's factory - seen on the far left - survived the war unscathed, and its 220ft chimney was one of Bristol's most familiar landmarks until the building was demolished in 1961. The long building nearer to us is Electricity House. The spires and towers of many churches point heavenwards in this view: on the left behind Electricity House is St John's of the Wall; further to the right, St Peter's, then St Mary le Port - both bombed during the war; moving on, the tall spire of Christ Church; All Saints; St Nicholas, destroyed by enemy bombs; Holy Cross, seen on the right near Temple Meads goods station, also bombed; the church of St Thomas a Beckett, now closed, lies nearby, and nearer to us we see the elegant tower of St Stephens, with the offices of the Evening World nearby. St Mary's on the Quay is just off-centre in the foreground. Trenchard Street cuts across the view from the right corner; the YMCA was later to replace some of these old buildings.

How many of our readers once rocked the night away in the old Byzantine granary? Remember those dances back in the 60s and 70s, and the marvellous music with a beat that stirred the blood and had us twisting to Chubby Checker tunes and rocking to the music made popular by the Rolling Stones and Status Quo? With a little persuasion, a few may even admit to having seen The Ladybirds in the far off days of their reckless youth. They were a lively girl band whose particular attraction is perhaps best left unmentioned.... The old granary was a fortunate survivor among the many buildings in Bristol which fell victim to the city planners, and has even been used in the popular TV series 'Only Fools and Horses'. Llandoger Trow, an old inn nearby in King Street, also survived. Welsh Back, whose name reminds us of the trade which once flourished between Bristol and South Wales, was one of the city's earliest quays. Modern office blocks have brought the waterside to life once more. Left of centre in this view, which dates from 31st May 1957.

MEMORIES OF BRISTOL

The Tower of St Mary Redcliffe is the vantage point that gives us this peep at Bristol as it was in the mid 1950s. Looking up Redcliffe Hill - towards Bedminster, a number of long vanished and sadly half-forgotten landmarks draw our eye: to the right of centre in the distance, the old Zion Chapel, today the Area Housing Office, and to the right of that, WD & HO Wills' factory, which once provided employment in the tobacco industry for thousands of Bristolians, and would make way for the Asda superstore. It was the Wills family whose generosity helped to found Bristol University. Insurance offices would one day replace the parade of shops on the right. Remember the faggot shop, whose chitterlings were to die for? And the old Ship Inn? All gone. Pets' Paradise, at the far end of the row of shops, would supply your pets with baskets, collars, leads, and anything else to do with feeding, rearing and training them. The first of the new flats can be seen on the left; the Redcliffe flats were yet to be built across the road.

MEMORIES OF BRISTOL

Peace had come to Bristol after six long years of war, and these buildings in Queen's Road, pictured in November 1946, had managed to survive the worst of the bombing raids. The names above the shops on the left will ring many bells among our older readers who will remember Fortts, whose delivery van stands at the ready, Lalondes estate agents, Bristol Wireless, and Brights' department store. Bristol Wireless, who advertised themselves as 'wireless and TV specialists', were established in Bristol back in 1922. Brights were to be taken over by the House of Frazer, become Dingles - and eventually close their doors at the end of the 20th Century. And remember Buxton's chemists shop? Their canopy can be seen on the opposite side of the road.

MEMORIES OF BRISTOL

By 1966, changes on a small scale - and on the large - were well advanced in Bristol. From the closing down of small shops such as Maynards, where we used to buy our midget gems and liquorice allsorts, to the opening of pizza, kebab, and other fast food outlets in the Centre, constant change is here to stay. Postwar university buildings - the schools of Engineering, Chemistry and Medicine - shape the skyline, with the Royal Fort jutting up halfway along. The Hippodrome, as important a part of Bristol's history as any other, has, by the date of the photograph, lost its familiar globe and its upper storey; the theatre remains an important entertainments centre. Colston Hall, to the rear of the Wessex coaches booking office, is also thankfully still with us.

The lighted Christmas tree in College Green back in 1958 provides a beautiful backdrop to this scene of the very first Christmas, and mothers have brought their children to gaze in wonder at the crib, and the young mother Mary and her child, the son of God whose first home was a stable and whose bed was a manger. The crib served to remind passers by that though they might not count themselves well to do, there were many in the city who could only look forward to a very lean Christmas. Gifts were being collected on the day of the photograph to pass on to children who would otherwise be forgotten by Santa.

Whether your seat was a wooden 'park' bench or simply the low wall bordering the now non existent flower beds, lingering in Broad Quay with the sun on your face was one of life's simple pleasures as Spring bloomed again after a long, cold winter. All seemed well, on this bright Wednesday morning, and every available seat in the semicircle around the Neptune statue appears to be filled. The Centre is an area which has been transformed almost beyond recognition since the late 1950s; only Neptune remains constant. Cast in lead, the ancient Roman 'god of the sea' was installed, together with his own fountain, in Temple Street back in 1723. After a number of moves, in 1949 Neptune was given a permanent home and a granite plinth at St Augustine's bridgehead.

At leisure

A sight we will never see again - a ship tied up at St Augustine's Bridge! This charming photograph dates from June 1935, a year before work began on covering in this stretch of the River Frome. The equipment may have changed, but an ice cream seller was as popular then as now, and an indulgent grandad has dipped into his pocket and bought his little grandaughter an ice cream cone. The view captures the Hippodrome, boasting a generous 'three hours programme'. Built as a variety theatre, the Hippodrome was massive, with a luxurious 2,000 seat auditorium with stalls, circle and gallery, and a state of- the-art dome which could be opened for ventilation. By 1930, however, the lure of moving pictures was beginning to outpace live theatre, and after the runaway success of an experimental 2-week showing of 'Congorilla', the Hippodrome dedicated itself wholly to the 'silver screen' in September 1932.

MEMORIES OF BRISTOL

A trestle table set up on an old bomb site and a talent for fast talking that would attract the punters; these were the basic ingredients for earning yourself a bob or two on the side. And if, added to that, you had a pack of cards in your pocket and an aptitude for sleight of hand, your success was guaranteed. 'Find the lady' may well have been the game in progress here in Fairfax Street back in 1955. It looked easy: keep your eye fixed on the queen, note where the man put it, and put your money on one of the three cards. Then, unbelievably, he would turn up the five of clubs or some other card and say, 'Unlucky, sir - you missed out there.' Your money was whisked away and you were left wondering how in the world you could have been mistaken; after all, you had actually seen the queen as he placed it on the table! It was clever stuff, and drawing a crowd was simple. A couple of mates standing around to win a game or two would swiftly pull in others to watch and see how easy it was to gain a little extra cash.

The Saturday matinee where, for just a few coppers, we could see one of the popular cartoons, a couple of feature films, and exciting trailers of forthcoming films to entice us back time and again. Roy Rogers and his faithful Trigger; the Lone Ranger; Superman; the dog Lassie - they were all there. The whole programme was punctuated by cheers and jeers, flying bits of rubbish, the popping of bubble gum, the 'oohs' of excitement, and the shouts of 'Put a penny in!' that harassed the long suffering projectionist when the film broke, as frequently happened. The Carlton cinema in Westbury on Trym was a popular cinema in its day, and its 820 seat auditorium was often well filled, a ground level cafe adding to its appeal. 'The Reluctant Debutante' was being screened at the time of the photograph. The days of the old Carlton were already numbered, however; it was pictured here in April 1959 not long before it closed and the site was later redeveloped as Westbury's new shopping centre.

On the move

Men and women in hats and suits, long dark coats, and heavy dresses. Was this photograph, then, taken on a chilly February day? Not a bit of it. This was Bristol Bridge on 13th July 1938. If these people could only see us now, what would they think of the short shorts, bare legs, naked midriffs and pierced navels on show in our 21st century summers? Tramcar No 19, here advising us to eat Harris's sausages, would, with the rest of the fleet, have given place to the motor bus and disappeared from our streets by 1941; and what about the prominent advertisement on the right? The sweeping claim that 'Germolene heals all skin trouble' is one which would doubtless be questioned today!

KNOWLE
HARRIS
WILTSHIRE
SAUSAGES
GINGER ALE
B&P
Heals
ALL SKIN
TROUBLE
OINTMENT
Touch!
oughs Colds & Bronchitis
THE GREAT FAMILY REMEDY!
19

MEMORIES OF BRISTOL

It's March 1938, and the winter is only just past, but even so the crisp, bright sunshine has tempted a couple of passengers on to the top deck of this Bristol tram. The drivers were even worse off than the passengers. They were provided with leather aprons as protection from the weather, but we can imagine what a comfortless job tram driving would have been in a harsh winter. In the year of the photograph motor buses began to take over as the old trams were phased out. But when war broke out trams were kept in service until a bomb severed the power cables in 1941, leaving only two workable routes. It was the end of the line for Bristol's trams.

MEMORIES OF BRISTOL

One-horse-power replaces the internal combustion engine in this wartime image, reminding us that petrol was precious and strictly rationed at the time. 'Give us the tools - we will finish the job,' reads the notice in the rear window, repeating the words of Winston Churchill to President Roosevelt in a radio broadcast in February that same year. This was 'War Weapons Week', held in July 1941 to encourage people to put their money into National Savings. War Weapons Week in 1941, Warships in 1942, Wings for Victory in 1943 and Save the Soldier in 1944. These special events raised thousands of pounds for the war effort, but more importantly people felt that they were doing their part. The war effort prompted much rivalry between local companies; the larger ones might raise £20,000 for a Wellington Bomber (to be repaid after the war). Many towns and cities actually 'bought' Spitfires for £5,000.

MEMORIES OF BRISTOL

Cars parked in the bus stands in Colston Street? This strange scene, caught on camera on 23rd July 1957, is one which was echoed in many towns and cities across Britain back in the 1950s, and its cause was a walkout by bus drivers and conductors. The strike made it difficult to find a parking place in the city, and these smart car owners who nabbed the bus stands were the lucky ones. If you owned a car in the 1950s you were fortunate indeed; other commuters had to brush off the dust and pump up the tyres of their old push bikes, while even more were reduced to 'shanks's pony'. However sympathetic the commuters were with the demands of the busmen, that did not solve their immediate problem, which was to get to and from work. The Thatcher Government of the 1980s introduced measures to curb trade unions' power to strike, and in 1984 an Act was passed that made a secret ballot of members obligatory before a strike.

MEMORIES OF BRISTOL

A holiday feeling is in the air as long queues form at the bus stands in Colston Avenue. It's Whit Monday 1955 - 30th May - and while the girls in their teens and 20s are out in their flowered summer dresses, the older ladies are playing safe and sticking with their more sensible coats. Churches often held special Whit Sunday services to mark Pentecost, and while for large numbers of people Whit Monday simply meant a day's holiday from their working life, many churchgoers were gathering for their annual 'Whit Walk'. Every church in the community would unite to progress through the local streets, each behind their individual banner, all marching in step behind a rousing band. The Whitsuntide procession is a long established tradition in Kingswood (and is still carried on today).

MEMORIES OF BRISTOL

Traffic chaos at Bristol Bridge: Most of us think of traffic jams and congested town centres as a relatively new experience, but not so! This picture taken in 1937 shows that Bristol had its problems so long ago. The scene is Bristol Bridge and queues like this were commonplace until Redcliffe Way was built to ease the situation. The Fry's van must have been making deliveries to local stores of such delights as chocolate cream bars, Turkish delight, Crunchie bars and 'Five Boys' chocolate.

Shopping spree

The well-stocked windows of Strode Cosh & Penfold have enticed a couple of young ladies to stand and gaze, and hopefully choose and buy! The scene was captured in April 1957; the war had been over for a decade, all rationing had finally ended in July 1954. As we can see, fashion too had been affected by the atmosphere of plenty; gone were the skimpy lines of utility clothing, and Dior's generous 'Aline', launched in 1955, is reflected in the clothing of these young women. Strode Cosh & Penfold's was, as readers may remember, much more than your average chemist's shop! Their building on the corner of Broadmead and Lower Union Street was only three years old at the time of the photograph, and was destined to stand for less than half a century.

MEMORIES OF BRISTOL

The market in High Street was always a good starting place for the housewives of Bristol, who week after week would catch a bus into town and tour the market to find the best - and cheapest - fruit and vegetables. April 1938, when this picture was taken was not the most affluent of times for the ordinary person in the street. The lady with the open shopping basket pictured here with her husband would perhaps shop around and buy potatoes and cabbage from one stall, carrots and a swede from another and, if the housekeeping money would stretch to it, maybe a pound of apples and a few bananas from a third. The war years saw bananas disappear from our shops, not to reappear until 1946. Children born during the war had never seen a banana, and had no idea that they had to peel off the skin before they could eat the fruit. The Home Secretary actually went on the radio, giving children instructions how they should open and eat them!

As if we were not already aware of the nature of Carwardine's business, the window display of tea pots and coffee-making accessories says it all, and on a pleasant day in the late 1950s, the gaily striped awning shades the windows of one of Bristol's most well known coffee bars from the sunshine. Carwardine's was a popular place to meet friends, and three elderly ladies, in their smart suits and neat little hats - the badge of the 1950s - step out briskly towards the doorway. Carwardine's coffee bar was on the corner of Horsefair and Lower Union Street. Earlier years had seen a watering hole of quite a different character in this position when the old Haymarket Tavern still stood, catering for Bristolians' thirst. The pleasant Victorian pub was lost to the city during the post-war redevelopment of Bristol. The shop premises across the road were to be given a facelift in the 1980s.

Though it is only 9.30 in the morning, this group of Bristol housewives look weary already. It was April 1964, and with domestic freezers still a luxury item which few could afford, the woman of the house still had to shop for fresh food several times a week. Cater, Stoffell & Fortt was a favourite port of call; our readers will perhaps remember the old traditional grocery store with a touch of nostalgia. Even the little dog in the photograph - whose mistress obviously shopped here - looks well fed and happy! Bacon, sliced as you wanted it by one of those dangerous looking machines; cheese soft and hard, mild Cheddar or Blue Stilton; 'best' butter or Stork margarine; garlic sausage or slices of salami; and eggs large and small, each with a little lion stamped on it. 'Go to work on an egg,' the British Egg Marketing Board encouraged us from 1957 onwards, together with the slogan 'You can rely on the Lion'. The lion stamp was removed from eggs at the end of 1968.

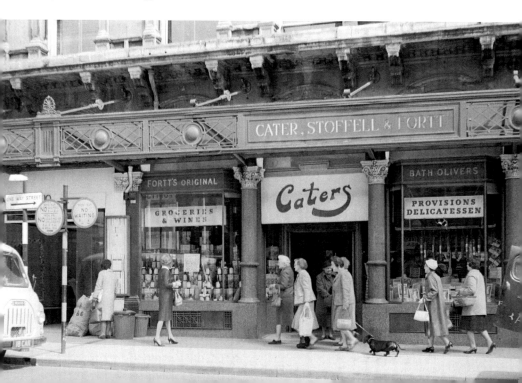

With very special thanks and appreciation for their help and contribution:

Reece Winstone Archive

Local Studies Section at Bristol Central Library

Martyn Hunt